# CHERISHING LIFE CHERISHING MYSELF

POETRY KHAKHOLIA MUNDRA

ISBN 979-888591883-1

Poetry Khakholia Mundra

## About the author

*She is Poetry Khakholia Mundra, 43 years old, married since seventeen years, having two children, living in the midst of hills and dales, valley and mountains, the land of Goddess Kamakhya, Guwahati Assam.*
*Her mother name is Deepa Devi Khakholia,*
*Her father name is Debi Prasad Khakholia. She is fourth in her family, of five children and is much attached with all her brothers and sisters..*
*She has done Mcom, Med and LLB, honours in management was lecturer in the university for sometimes. But that never gave her the tranquil she was looking for, and life has so much for her in the basket, that she started expressing and weaving her thoughts and feelings into her own words..*
*She has done around more than 200 anthologies, and one compilation too .. named*
*"Undying Emotions"*

*Her two solo books were launched, back to back this January, in Hindi and English namely,*
हमारी जदिंगी हमारे एहसास *under (Life World Community)*
*My Book of Untold Emotions under ( Writers Hub Publication)*
*She is also the Writer Admin and Ambassador of*

*Sparkling Cornexpress community...*
*Besides she has won more than 500 certificates, trophy and medals respectively, in most writing community. Also participated in many open mics, jugalbandi, and has won considerably..*
*She is an active writer at your quote app, with the id : Befikr lafz, under pen name: Soulful love.. There she has written around more than 4000 quotes and poems... And is now, all set to publish her books, and stories under different banners and publication houses...*
*Besides, her work is published monthly in the international magazine Namaste India..*
*Most prominently her name is listed in India's Top 25 Deserving Writers...*
*She is both a bilingual and an erotica writer which is her USP too.... She loves to play, rhyme and chyme with words in her own chords.. Last but not the least she is a tea and music lover whose only abode is peace and empathy.*
*Her motto in life is to*
*Live and let live*
*Love and let love..*

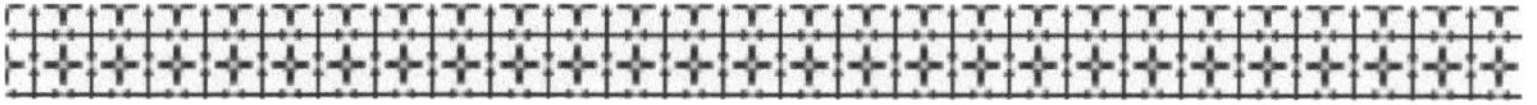

## About the Book

*Cherishing Life Cherishing myself*
*is a book carrying the many beautiful times, memories and*
*my attachment with people surrounding me and*
*outshining my*
*vision and valour to*
*peace and bliss..*
*This book is in short, the sum total of my choices and*
*decisions, my likes and dislikes for some particular thing*
*or people.. and opinions generated duly..*
*While at the same time cherishing me and instilling the*
*motivation to go beyond the inconsistencies of lives and*
*come out as unchallenged star in myraids, in the sky, that*
*is always blue for me, but now, sky seems to be green and*
*gay,*
*fuller and rewarding enough..., to appreciate the beauty*
*beneath beguiles of the yesteryears...!!*

# Contents

# Contents

# 1. Journey of my writing

*I never thought of becoming a writer myself although in school I used to prepare notes of all subjects and scored well too. Then in the later phase of my college days wrote some articles and got published in the daily newspaper just thinking that I could become a journalist but in those days in 2001 talking about, journalism was not considered a professional course or so and people used to laugh at me so I had to abandon my thinking of journalism as also no course was available on good grounds and finally ended up doing Bcom, B.ed, Mcom, Llb after marriage and writing got stuck somewhere down the woods and goods of the family found too much entangled in house and children so had to leave my job of a lecturer to homemaker.*

*But destiny has many facets and it takes you to places that were meant for you only, same happened to me. And I again started writing articles poems and quotes but in my copy and till today many copies are filled with my thoughts pouring out all my emotions under one banner.*

*Nevertheless, nothing much was happening except that I used to write my feelings on finding a writing group called poetry lovers but not satisfied feeling a void, still to be filled. Then suddenly one day, my daughter and my niece struck me with the idea of writing on the app called your quote because my niece was already familiar there, had herself wrote many quotes, etc with beautiful backgrounds ... and soon they both were ready with my new I'd pic, etc to explore the world of writings thoughts feelings on different notes and background evoked my senses to experience a completely new me...*

*And this is how a by the chance coincidence of my niece who was on this same app, your quote suggested my name to be here, for she liked my writings a lot. From here my writing journey took another leap which was otherwise, confined to my room and filling heavy copies with thought-provoking editorials, poems, quotes shares etc.*

*And today I'm here doing several anthologies covering almost all genres, bilingual writer too I'm, sees no inhibitions to writing my mind, heart and soul for reader to acknowledge me and see through of the world with a different perspective of love, romance, heartbreak sadness, dejection loneliness, seductions passions and pleasures beyond all lies one hidden heart full of desires unleash satiation.*

*Hence this is just a beginning of my journey full of rifts and rides roses and writhes but I'm optimistic to make a mark upon my reader who will finally shower me applause and accolades, the success of many successes, for generations to cherish and nourish my name, no wonder , I'm living my name, that my mother gave, for she loved poetry, then she too wouldn't know that one day, I would actually be a living legend whose name carries her identity, her passionate soul and cravings to write ponder and yonder beyond horizons...!!*

*By : Poetry Khakholia Mundra*

*Insta I'd: _befikr_lafz*

# 2. letter to yourself

*Dear me,*

*You had always been your favourite, though I was shy, but a happy go lucky person always, this is the real you, who spread happiness and joy wherever you go, try soaring in goodness and mercy, for forgive and forgiveness is your motto, however or how many times people hurt you, misunderstood and misappropriated your conduct, they one day, had to realise and repent for not believing in you, your benevolence ultimately speaks your uniqueness.*

*So just stick to it never let loose yourself for anyone, have faith in the Almighty and live to the fullest without ever compromising your freedom at all, for thats what define you as a being, a fuller being a self made independent identity you are and shall remain so ever and ever...!!*

*By : Poetry Khakholia Mundra*

*(Mcom, Med, LLB)*

*Freelance Bilingual Writer*

*Insta I'd: _befikr_lafz*

# 3. Why I write

*Writing is the innate self of self, which pours out one's true self from the hidden arenas of conscious and subconscious state of mind...*
*In this very context I would say that I write priorly because I love to write my thoughts and feelings so as to shape me stronger than ever..*
*I write for myself particularly to be at peace, tranquility persists towards pleasure and passions.. This soothes and smoothers me from within to curb all my negativity and anger which I definitely succumbs as any natural being..*
*For writing gives me my happiness and solace to go beyond my imagination and creativity to play the words as we play flute so innocently so subtly until we attain expertise in it..*
*However writing is a never ending process sailing in the minds rolling in the hearts like sea waves on the sea shore never to forget their inherent nature of swaying whirling and dashing the shore of the sea just as a writer never stops penning a simple thought...!!*
*Alas writing is actually God's grace and grandeur to connect to Him and to the world around, through myraids of words, like stars in the sky sparkling and glittering in the glory of beauty...!!*
*By : Poetry Khakholia Mundra*
*Insta I'd: _befikr_lafz*

# 4. From dawn to dusk

*There was a time*
*when i used to be called*
*a tubelight in everything*
*i did never ever anyone thought how I felt it*
*what scars it imprinted on my naive mind..*
*This was my past dark and delusioned..*
*Grew up to be the same*
*always being dependent , disappointed with myself*
*like good for nothing, am i, bore this mindset..., looped me, in utter agony*
*forlorn, dejected, rejected lot,*
*like none surmised my immature soul, so pure, so lethargic, swayed*
*by outside whims and fancies, but things prove me wrong sometimes...*
*Now I'm candid, self dependent, outspoken.., straight forward person*
*from being the tubelight, silent to fierce one, the*
*journey wasn't so good.., had many upheavals,*
*croosroads to be passed stones to be crushed,*
*crushing me inner, many times, but i stood for myself, I cared for my existence, not always to*
*be drifted, by the winds of pressure, people and policing..., but became a storm forbidden and*
*forsaken and a living legend for all, enshrined beauty, I'm today....!!*
*By: Poetry Khakholia Mundra*
*Insta I'd:_befikr_lafz*

# 5. Love with Books

*Books are the mirror image of our society.*
*Books enlighten us rejuvenate us and are a source of solace.*
*When one is low, lonely and lethargic books can relish his anxiety his pain and comfort him from all mundanity and mess of the life and of living.*
*That's why it is sometimes said that books are better teachers, friend, philosopher and guide...*
*I love to spend wholesome time reading books of my choice, which includes both motivational and romantic ones. One of my all favourite book is Be at your best.. which in an insight into your own self, choices and identities to be yourself first..very soothing and heartening..*
*Hence i personally believe that, books like our teacher teach us, guide us, help us and reduce our stress and strain of lives..*
*A good book or reading a book of one's own choice acts as healthy motivator, instills in me confidence, adding juices to my otherwise monotonous life, or may do so to anyone who loves to read books..*
*Teachers may not be always there with us but books are our forever friends, is rightly said....!*
*Books are the soul laminator tuning us in both good and bad times.*
*Without books our life would be dull or like a ruderless ship aiming nowhere.*
*So it is the books which build castles and creates magic in the hearts of millions from darkness to hope and light, and towards one's own progressive future.*
*By: Poetry Khakholia Mundra*

*Insta I'd: _befikr_lafz*

# 6. Angel of my life

*I dedicate this title to one and only my eldermost sister, who is such a soulful person, in herself.*
*Being in the noblest profession, she already has won the hearts of many downtrodden and sick people suffering beyond agonies.*
*Yes she is a doctor who surpasses all while treating her patients like a family and for me the angel, the sunshine, my rainbow, who bring hope and exuberance to my otherwise, lonely, desolate and painful life.*
*She is more of a troubleshooter for me in any problem as the, moment i encounter, she comes as the sole saviour and solves in seconds, my turmoils like god's messenger, sent especially, for me for erasing all my anguish and aggression towards life and living..,alas always underestimating myself and rebuking*
*God for not giving a fuller, happier life, for always being fantasizing love and life on my ways.*
*But it's my sister who consoles and paves an easier and smoother paths, for me and does all she can, to make me from remorse to rejoice.*
*She is truly the angel for many, but for me the rainbow of my life, spreading all the colours of life, love, hope, happiness, beauty and a lustrous living fulfilling enriching myself beyond the mirrors.*
*By : Poetry Khakholia Mundra*
*Insta I'd: _befikr_lafz*

# 7. Memories of school

*School life is brighter beautiful but at the same time with lots of criss cross and rifts though posing threat to adjustment and compromises yet soothing and remembering experiences endured over the times.*

*So in this very context I am narrating a real incident of my student life which was pathetic, yet unperished memories touched beyond years ...*

*This is the incident when I was in class 9, was quite a good student but was not good in maths still tried hard to get marks fair enough. Also my maths teacher didn't like me or nor did i liked her instead was scornful, because she always scolded me for no reasons.*

*In our times we had weekly test every Saturday and this time it was maths test of 50 marks in which I scored barely 14 marks not even passed, and i cried like anything, because never such low marks I got ever, above when i went for correction got scolding too, from the ever barbaric maths teacher... that don't compare, this was very common those days for teachers to skip giving marks .*

*Alas! I could do nothing then crying and rebuking the teacher like hell. But what I did which was very unexpected for me or for anyone to believe that I tore that paper in my anger and frustration. But marks are to be added and verified for final result but what would i do now, can't take the blame upon myself either so made a story that rats ate the test paper, since we had ration shop and there were many rats roaming up and down ...So it was quite easy to wrap a story of my torn maths test paper.*

*When I told my teacher she didn't believe, first she laughed, then the whole class started laughing, making fun and alas, the maths teacher*

*scolded me like anything. I couldn't take this and didn't go to school for two days in pain and anguish....and laments.*
*Whereas my class teacher was very nice she finally called my twin sister asking me to come to school and speak up my heart to her. I was full of hope and told her everything the whole truth that I only tore the paper out of anger for scoring so low. She consoled me and told never to repeat this mistake in future and shall sort out everything with the maths teacher herself., and that she wouldn't scold me now..*
*I always admired my class teacher she was my english teacher very dignified, very disciplined yet understanding and soulful.So, because of her I could come out of this bad experience and finally scored well when that haughty maths teacher left after few months.*
*I thanked God for she was like on my head always rebuking and scolding me and till opposite of was the English teacher whom I admire and cherish even today, though, she is no more and I owe my English learning to her solely, love her indepth...!!*
*By: Poetry Khakholia Mundra*
*Insta I'd: _befikr_lafz*

# 8. My brother is like

*My brother is like*
*my friend with whom i*
*can talk freely, though*
*he is the eldest yet the most*
*loved one who gets*
*annoyed like a child, for he*
*is a bit bossy and attention*
*seeker, but we cherish him*
*for all his benevolence and*
*greatfulness towards all,*
*for he is a passionate soul,*
*in all his doings and keeping*
*up with relations.*
*He is my motivation too.*
*I call him my Big B and love him*
*a lot revere him a lot...!!*
*By: Poetry Khakholia Mundra*
*Insta I'd: _befikr_lafz*

# 9. Subject I dislike

*Subjects are many, which we come across in our school and college life.. Some we like, others we are not much interested but there is that one particular subject which we wholly dislike...*
*And this one hateful subject for me is none other than Maths, not that i hated it purposely or intentionally, rather this hatred and dislike developed over the years , because of the inability to grasp the concepts, seemingly tough and stuck me leading to nowhere, however hard i tried to...*
*Maths always left me aghast, doldrums and in dilemma, eventually frustrating with my own self when unable to understand the numbers, algebraic expressions, geometry, trigonometry, theorems, making me ponder why we need to solve all this..*
*Most importantly, why should i find the value of x, or y when they never seemed so simple..*
*The rules, diagrams, graphs, bar diagrams, unitary and other methods never gave me logical solution and i could never decipher them. I always fought my inner self while solving maths problem.*
*Also i feared my maths teacher a lot, she would rebuke me for no or for sillly reasons, i was also horrified by her that also kept me at a backfoot in this subject, always trying to escape from her clutches..,who was like head on heels.*
*Alas! I could never get a good maths teacher except my own home tutor, who made things clear and simpler for me, that i could pass out matriculation scoring good marks mostly in all the subjects, latter marks*

*in English, but maths that average only.., when i expected quite more. So however hard i try or give my best to this one subject, i know i won't make it. Also lack of interest and fear are yet another reasons for my dislike...,for interest come with proper guidance and enthusiasm to learn but sadly for maths, i could never say this..!!*

*By : Poetry Khakholia Mundra*

*Insta I'd: _befikr_lafz*

# 10. Celebrity I would like to meet

*Celebrities are many who truly deserves accolade for their ingenius contribution to the fields they belong or are actually born to be there only.. One such celebrity whom I adore and enamour till today is none other than the heart throb of many also, atleast if not today, then in our times, he was the most romantic hero the Indian film industry ever produced.. Yes , he is none other than one and only Badshaah of Bollywood King Khan.. Shahrukh Khan, who is my all time favourite film star ..*
*From my school days especially when his blockbuster movie Ddlj hit the cinema screen, though I liked him from before , but this one movie changed his life and my admiration for him, that till today after years when so many other new comers have joined the battlefield, no wonder he continues to steal the hearts of many .*
*Even my own niece is her fan when she saw Shahrukh in so many good movies.. I'm so much attracted towards him that even wrote a poem on him and so only is desirous that , if one day by chance , I get to meet my favourite, my wonderstruck star Shahrukh Khan , then I shall surely read my poem written especially for him with much love and romance unleashing me..*
*For romance is catapulated and captivated by him only . He took romance to different realms of life..*
*With his ever charming way of hands wide open and enchanting her woman like*

*heavenly desires and that his and mine too favourite lines..*
*Kuch kuch hota hai*
*Anjali, tum nhi samjhogi... So I feel that if I meet him someday then might request to say the same line for me, this is too much expecting may be, but I know he is a divine romantic soul and shall surely fulfill my wish..*
*Oh..! I'm completely mesmerized in his thoughts of love and passion, a feeling of my joy and pride alike, which I want to live once atleast before I die..!!*
*By : Poetry Khakholia Mundra*
*Insta I'd: _befikr_lafz*

# 11. Life Partner

*That one movie that is forever green in my memory and that touched my heart, my life and soul is life partner starring Govinda and other are fardeen Khan, Genelia, Prachi Desai, Tushar kapoor etc etc*
*This movie is the reality of married life and of married couples, their ups and downs after marriage be it arranged or love, life turns upside down after marriage, for marriage is not a bed of roses and if we don't realise this reality to shoulder the responsibility befalling marriage, it harshly turmoils the couples and their marriage resulting in divorce and separation.*
*Patience, perseverance faith and understanding are the keynotes of a married life, and most touching was the dialogue that out of the three couples one says who did love marriage, whose life was very happenning and blissful when lovers but things changed after marriage.*
*The lover now turned husband Fardeen Khan says to his girlfriend Genelia now wife, that... Sanjana tum kab badi hogi ab bhi agar tum girlfriend hi bani rahogi to hamare rishte se badbu aane lagegi...*
*Its high time u stop behaving like a girlfriend and start sharing home responsibility as wife.. This is so true for we girls who become women soon after marriage, and whole lot expectations fall flat on our naive shoulders, which both the couples should balance and harmonize, and with negotiations and novelty blended in love, so as to have a happy and a peaceful married life..!!*
*By: Poetry Khakholia Mundra*
*Insta I'd: _befikr_lafz*

# 12. My favourite Song

*Songs are many, soulful, thrilling and soothing too..*
*Likewise all are good ones hinting, touching our untold emotions, connected with our own lives..., somewhere, deep down the memory lane...*
*I kind of like musical hindi notes, but that one song which touched my life, my emotions immeasurably is the hindi movie Kabir Singh song kaise hua, kaise hua tu itna jaruri kaise hua...,*
*I simply love this song and listen always, but never get bored, for each time i listened to it, i connect so well, getting positive vibes from this song that dwells the spirit , hope and a feeling of bliss that how one person becomes so important in our life.., that you can't do without him and life becomes so beautiful, so rosy and happening with him, thinking, surmising in his love, his lusts, his crusts, and his soul needs you, and you need him..*
*That's the best thing about this song that it is full of love and life..., and that what we actually miss in our actual lives..., no matter how much we achieve, but we want this true love of someone who constantly thinks, ponder, and yonder you and you only..*
*You mean everything to him.*
*You are his world...*
*Thats the beauty, the bliss and ecstasy of this song and i love it all..!!*
*By : Poetry Khakholia Mundra*
*Insta I'd: _befikr_lafz*

# 13. Favourite flower

*Flowers are many in the garden of life, but one whose essence, sweetness and attraction lures me more towards it, is none, other than, Rose the king of flowers.., the flower of beauty and love.. yes its a red rose indeed, which i like the most.*

*I'm very much enticed by this one flower which actually i expect to get everyday from my husband..*

*But he has become a bit miser after marriage, and have stopped giving me red rose, not a single one while, he used to give me everyday before marriage..*

*So whenever i see my favourite flower , i remember my good old days, when he used to come with a red rose in his hand for me always,*

*the aroma, the colour red adds to its ecstatic beauty, and the moment he gave me, my eyes sparkled bright and beautiful, ready to fall into his arms..*

*I love red rose from very beginning when i learnt the concept of flowers..,*

*No wonder i cherish tulips, lily, sunflower too, but my love and lusts for this one flower is beyond any one's imagination..!!*

*By : Poetry Khakholia Mundra*

*Insta I'd: _befikr_lafz*

# 14. Writing my habit, and hobby

*Writing is my passion, pride, my pastime also the favourite art, blend in bliss and fulfillment, positivity, accolades my heart and soul...*
*I never thought, could write my feelings, words weaved in words, feelings poured in verses and thoughts symbolized..*
*More so, never ever thought of living my name as such, which is indeed God's true blessings upon me...*
*I love to play with words, in rhythmic delights, and pleasurable musical notes, flowing like rivulets in its own kingdoms of realms and rejoice ...*
*Moreover, its still more cherishing that I'm a bilingual as well as an erotica writer, who try, and can bring out the most innate desires, knit lustily as if, one living the moment itself, filled with romance, beauty, passions unleashed of any man's happiness, though hidden, emotions ,,,,, under his sleeves, beyond the years of glory and grandeur ... Alas! wants are insatiable and limitless just like writing.*
*So i love to entwine myself in writing on every genres, that may touch human lives and drives to eternity...!!*
*By : Poetry Khakholia Mundra*
*Insta I'd: _befikr_lafz*

# 15. Events that brought immense happiness

*This is not confined to merely one event, because that one event is yet to come in my life, i hope so, but till then upto this day, if i would recall then there are some events, precious and memorable to my heart, that also brought immense happiness as well.*

*One such event is when i got best girl position for class 6, a certificate and my first trophy even, was quite unexpected in a convent, when competition was too high, but God blessed me with this immense happiness..*

*Another was when i scored latter marks in English, and made a leap from 59% to 70% in matriculation exams, when in those days passing, was a hullabaloo, and very tough in our Assam State board..*

*However, after this followed many more events which had a mixed blend of joys and happiness ...*

*But then yet another event was when i passed LLB scoring good marks and then 8.1cgp in my Mcom, was quite a moment of joviality and blissfulness in my life, that i could surpass all of these exams fairly, and upto my expectations, when in those days, it was so very unexpecting of a girl to study so higher in our community...*

*Last but not the least, when i got job in a college, for the first time i would be teaching a class full of big students, putting forth many challenges as well an amazing experiences of head and heart, proving my calibres simultaneously, an edge over me.....*

*But now, im waiting for that one moment of happiness, no wonder my joy, my mirth, my solace are all, i seek, in my children, who are actually the whole source of my happiness above all the happiness of the world...!!*

*By : Poetry Khakholia Mundra*

*Insta I'd: _befikr_lafz*

# 16. Coffee with Poetry

*We have heard a lot*
*about coffee with karan....,*
*but never ever heard something, like coffee with poetry, because poetry loves tea, so coffee doesn't get a chance...*
*Infact, poetry can be well versed with coffee too, because poetry can accommodate all drinks*
*be it tea, wine or coffee.*
*Poetry, coffee and the taste delights the sipper, what a blend of crush...,*
*like a school boy having his first crush on his teacher....!!*
*Name : Poetry Khakholia*
*Instagram id : _befikr_lafz*

# 17. Train Journey memories forever

*Long time back, i journeyed by train and enjoyed a lot with my family and co passengers, seen how the passersby keep moving trailing the whole boogie, how the vendors*
*trail shouting to sell their stuffs, above the beggars pleading in their horrible*
*voice singing, some melodies on a tanpura or so..*
*All these are worth watching and waiting till your stop comes.*
*Train journey is full of criss- cross, with safety at stake, for any carelessness may land you up in mishap of a lifetime...., But still the journey is interesting and challenging as well as interactive ,*
*as u get varied people and variety of experiences of a lifetime,*
*memories dwell all through out,*
*sometimes happy, sometimes hazy...!!*
*By : Poetry Khakholia Mundra*
*Insta I'd: _befikr_lafz*

# 18. My favourite colour

*Colours are many, varied and beautiful, enriching our lives with serenity and sensuality.*
*But my favourite colour is yellow, the colour of sunshine, the colour of sunflower, the colour of hope and light.*
*I rejuvenate, relish and relate to this very colour in most cases, which is my first choice in any case, no doubt.*
*Yellow is the colour of*
*joy and exuberance,*
*reverberating my life to optimism and enrichment, from the shackles of turmoils and*
*tarnishes, my pain soothes, the moment i*
*think of this colour, which sparkles the glory and grandeur, the beauty the galore, the ecstasy, as experiencing the brightest day of my life*
*as seeing the sun myself eye to eye captivates, enamours the living..*
*Yellow is also the symbol of friendships, torn between the terrains of life and living, still surmises the torments, stands tall beneath the beauty of friends, feeling of oneness, fraternity, fragility, no wonder, surpasses and rejuvenating the relationship in a bond beyond blood..*
*So yellow is colour of cherishing and rejoicing uplifting my life, redefining me, in many upheavels and untowardness, to look beyond the bliss and achieve the unachievable ever fulfilling and blooming like the sunflower blooms, like the sun shines bright*
*and beautiful,*
*heat and passions*

*reigning high and high*
*in the esctatic delights...!!*
*By : Poetry Khakholia Mundra*
*Insta I'd: _befikr_lafz*

# 19. Yes, im selfish

*Yes, I'm selfish*
*Yes, i dont and shouldn't*
*hesitate to admit that at times I'm selfish, for my own self, for satisfying my own desires and passions.*
*Yes I'm selfish when i stand for myself, for my sake, even against all, because i know myself the best, and so value myself to be what I'm and not to pretend, what i*
*ain't or what could become of me..*
*And i sincerely acknowledge that it's not bad or guilty to be selfish, if not hampering other's interest, feelings and emotions, rather protecting one's own self growth and respecting one's self confidence, is indispensable for a good life.. a cherished one indeed.*
*To be truthful, to be mature and to be at tranquil, being selfish is selflessness too at times. So I'm not*
*shy or wicked to admit that what I'm not, but accept with utmost pride and diligence that...,*
*Yes, I'm selfish, for*
*im a soulful person,*
*a human ultimately...!!*
*By : Poetry Khakholia Mundra*
*Insta I'd: _befikr_lafz*

# 20. Childhood toys

*Childhood is innocent*
*Childhood is naive and nice, but so are the toys with which we play along.*
*We didn't have teddy*
*We didn't have mobile*
*We didn't have videogames..either,*
*We didn't have gadgets unlike today's kids..*
*We had keys pulled toys the moment key stopped the toy stopped till we stopped clapping on its jerks and sounds. We made paper boats played with them under heavy downpours or under a bucket full of waters .*
*We made paper aeroplane which, we very, innocently, tried flying above the sky, but seldom succeeded.. a fuss on our faces yet shining and attempting futile though, that was our innocence wrapped in those many paper hand made toys..*
*We made paper lotuses paper roses, paper boats and paper fans in hundreds and sold out like any other today's businessman or woman. If nothing we got, to play then, would become vegetable vendors, collecting potato, onion, carrot, cabbage spinach tomato, etc etc from our mother's kitchen and sell it like any other today's vegetable vendors ....*
*Last not the least our toys, were our all day long gossips of school, and of passers by or the shops down the window, people staring we sisters above, giggling yet giving, tough looks, that make their eyes, go down in shy and shock. Nothing mattered us more than our incessant joys, laughter, fun and frolics in the innumerable competitions we played which today's kid*

*see on television like singing dancing, antakshri painting etc .*
*Alas we had lot more toys, than of today's kids. I really find them only between the gadgets, some may however, be innovative too, but still the race is on.. We were lucky in a way that we didn't have teddy*
*Or else would sleep by a teddy, instead, in delighful chitchatting with sisters.. So what we had, was priced possession.., Are treasures cherished forever, seldom detach, from bygone days, a thin attachment, still lingers, hard , can't let go off from the memories of the childhood...!!*

*By : Poetry Khakholia Mundra*
*Insta I'd: _befikr_lafz*

# 21. First Love or Crush

*I still remember, peeping , hiding myself, under the curtains of my small window, though large enough, for me to see him downstairs opposite to my house, sitting in his shop, dressed mostly in either white, or blue shirt, or t shirt and denims, very ordinary looking was he...*

*Yes dark complexion too, not very good height, and i was hardly in class seven or so, studying in a completely girl's school, was actually for the first time got attracted to him..*

*It was love or not or an infatuation might be but i kind of liked him like anything.*

*I used to wait for his shop to open, which usually opened at eight in the morning, generally, he only came first and i would peep through my window in the pretence of studying or watching the passersby..*

*He also used to see upstairs in my window, but never showed any signs as such, but i used to see him spend hours behind the curtains of the window..*

*Also when i used to go out, i wanted him to look at me and show some signs atleast, but it wasn't symbolic ever.., because sometimes he talked with me very normally and very little too..*

*Alas i would get annoyed if anyday he didn't come, or also when his shop closed at nine in the evening...*

*I always used to fantasize him with what thoughts that even i don't know now if i remember him, smile comes, because i had almost settled with him in my dreams, but he never showed any interest in me, and how could he for i was barely a class seven student , and he being in college....*

*He never felt for me the way i felt, but he was my first love for i waited for him like hell on my windows, wanted his one attention only..*
*He looked sometimes but never encouraged or encountered my feelings for him, that i don't know but i still mesmerize those bygone days of yesteryears, fond reminiscents, yet very heartfelt and sincere, no denying the fact that it was my first love until i could find my soulmate..*
*But first love is first only, none can replace it, nor the fond memories attached with it, that year after also we seek solace whatsoever, now through writing only, i seek relief and bliss...!!*
*By : Poetry Khakholia Mundra*
*Insta I'd: _befikr_lafz*

# 22. My Nightmares

*A mother is often in fear for her children that nothing bad happens to them ever, and if anything is destined to occur, then it should happen to her, not them..*

*Nightmares are really worst of human experiences that we often , or seldom, comes across, suddenly, or by chance, not by choice indeed. Similarly i ignore other nightmares at any point of day or night time, except the one, if ever, happen to see early in the morning, around 5 AM. This actually is my wrath and grief alike..*

*So once quite a long back not recently, I saw while i was waiting at the railway platform with my husband and children for our train to come, it was dark nearly. That after much a wait, the train came, rush ran all over the platform, people running like mad to catch before it leaves because not for long , the train stays in that station. So everyone needs to hurry and in haste, we however, kept the baggage and children also got up, in the train …… Only i was waiting down to get up soon, till then ,My husband settled the children , that time only train gave the horn. But he was inside the train, only i was in the platform standing , almost all had got up. And , i saw within no time, the train started to run, i was like yuck, what went wrong that day, my husband gave his hand, he couldn't jump also as the train was picking speed, and also children's safety was more important for me.*

*We both tried hard that i could catch the train, my children too yelling and screaming, husband tried and tried , alas ! I was in saree that finally while running, i stumbled and now my all hopes of being with my family dashed to ashes. I was literally in tears, for i was left alone in that abandoned deserted platform, the train had left leaving me in agony, aghast, aggrieved and in utter despair and gloom.. I now thought what will i do , but my husband could foresee and his last words were to go to the office and call home etc etc, hardly i heard half , as i was speechless, motionless when the moment i fell*

*i knew i had missed my train and now im all alone in this platform. This was indeed the worst nightmare, i had I don't know what i did after that, but yes my eyes opened, and i saw myself lying on the bed, beside my children.*

*I just thanked God for saving me, and later told this to my husband, he just laughed and whiled away in ignorance. But for me it was a horrified day, a gloomy night at the station, which could turmoil and shatter my entire life..!!*

*By : Poetry Khakholia Mundra*

*Insta I'd: _befikr_lafz*

# 23. my favourite writer

*To be very truthful*
*and candid I'm, then*
*I admit without, boast*
*that I like my writings,*
*I'm my own favourite*
*in respect of writing*
*my thoughts , feelings*
*of head and heart, my*
*words sometimes harsh*
*other times soothes me*
*and my readers alike..,*
*Sometimes corelate with*
*their lives inconsistent with the situation , however,*
*turmoils us a lot, in the many*
*realms of life..*
*Yet I pour my heart out my life, my rules, my vision, aspirations through my words.,*
*never to forsake , but to forget and forgive the incumbents, the perturbing elements of our lives, whom we can't avoid even.*
*So I write a mix blend of emotions dipped in love lusts, joy, mourn and sojourns of life. Perhaps, im no less than any other good writers so what's the harm if I'm my favourite so as to boost me instill the confidence, the charm and the glory . I inspire to aspire...*
*By : Poetry Khakholia Mundra*

*Insta I'd: _befikr_lafz*

# 24. Cultural exchange

*This is widely seen in our Indian heritage , where people from all caste, creed, colour, gender, religion etc comes in an unifying bond and togetherness to cherish and nourish the beauty of the cultures..*
*Likewise, I'm marwari so we have our own cultural entity and beauty and a lot many rites, rituals to be followed throughout the year. Starting with the Sankranti or the kite festival known mostly , where we offer 14 items to the poor and needy including the priests, after performing simple puja with sweets like gewar feeni, as bhog to the deity and as the delicacy of the festival.*
*Next comes the festival of colours, that is Holi , symbolizing the vadh of hriyanakashyap by his own son Prahlad and of holika dehan, the night before we play with gulal etc. Colours mark the spirit, spontaneity and seduction of this festival. Likewise we have many vrats too mention is Shivratri, karwa chout, janmastmi , ganesh chouth, and nine days worshipping of Durga MAA , is also patronised by us. Then there is Rakshabandhan , marking the bond between brother and sisters, no less than a festival for us, where the sister tie Rakhi on her brother's hand, andhaving sweets and gifts exchanged.*
*This is quite sacred and loving indeed, to see their love and protection ensured by the brother to his sister.*
*Janmastmi is yet, another beautiful occasion, more of a festival in our country, celebrating the birth of Lord Krishna, with much pomp and show, grace and glory, befitting the killing of his own mama kansh and freeing his parents from his shackles.. So bhogs are prepared which is*

*called panjiri, and dahi and dryfruits too , together with other sweets to the kanha. Also dahi handi is a very challenging ceremony type where a pyramid is made of people especially men only to break the handi pillared at a height. This is quite very exciting, enthusiastic where each one unites to celebrate the festival with oneness forgetting all their pains and grudges. Then for we married ladies, karwa chouth is also a festive occasion to seek god's blessing so as to have a happy married life by keeping whole day fast for the husband, wanting his longevity from God and family's happiness. Thereby breaking the fast after having seen and performed puja to the moon in the sky, when the moon also comes late that day to test our patience, beautifully attired sarees all indian women wait, for their moon to come , After this the husband himself serve water to his beautiful wife and then together they dine. This is no less than a festival for the indian married women across the country. There are yet many more festivals bringing the culture, the heritage, the ethnicity and the beauty of the holiness in each one, has its own unique significance of binding and unifying the indianess in all of us..!!*

*By : Poetry Khakholia Mundra*

*Insta I'd: _befikr_lafz*

# 25. Thankfulness

*Sometimes or say, very many times we forget to thank the many beautiful people out there in our lives.. Alas! I don't want to miss this opportunity before they bid or i might bade them goodbye for reasons beyond controls, or not, is quite unpredictable, atleast for now.. Hence, i very candidly affirm that its very important to show gratitude to all those associated with us in some or the other way.., SO ,*

*A note of thankfulness today, I give to all in true sense of the term..*

*Starting from the Almighty for giving me life and living for my survival and sustenance..*

*Then comes my parents who brought me into this world, fed me, and taught me to face the thick and thins of life, blended in virtues, deed and lessons on morality, beyond words, I could express.., even to make me good and a loving person ....*

*Nurtured and cared under them, made me more of a dependent which, I overcomed or was motivated by my husband, to do things beyond my destination.*

*So, I thank him, for building in a stronger me., inspite of being the mother of two children,*

*I stood like rock for them, this I owe to my husband only...*

*Last but not the least, I thank all my brothers and sisters who motivated and inspired me to do what I'm best at and sorting my problems every time... So whatever I'm today, is all because of my family and friends too, who in some or the other way either build walls or bridges for me eventually, making me grow stronger and stronger, facing the challenges with mighty hands.*

*Alas..! I thank my grandparents who are no more but their key goodness and spirit is still imbibed in me to attain my solace and success alike, their blessings I cherish till today ...!!*

***Thanku all***

*By : Poetry Khakholia Mundra*

*Insta I'd: _befikr_lafz*

# 26. A note to 2021

*The year 2021 was actually nothing more than the harbinger of 2020.*
*It had nothing of its own, or nothing new to give the world, or the people living, except to protect*
*oneself and take measures to safeguard from the havoc created by the pandemic..*
*So more sumptuously this year is the remnants of the 2020, healing, curing and enthralling us to get back to normal life, which was indeed a strong endeavour, a good motivator to give a fatal blow to this covid thing, which is in no way abandoning us.., except for the vaccines generated worlwide and precautions pronounced more deliberately..*
*Rest, i found nothing as of, yes to a great extent, the fear, the scorn we had in 2020, regarding the covid, the myths laiden so many shattering us wholly, succumbed to many houses and families.., was overcomed to some extent..*
*No wonder the lockdown , lessons taught immensenly, leaving many everlasting experiences, reduced paradigms to health , education and other sectors duly..*
*So i believe that the upcoming year may have its own uniqueness bringing new hopes, aspirations and happiness in each one's life , making us forget the forlorns of yesteryears....*
*By : Poetry Khakholia Mundra*
*Insta I'd: _befikr_lafz*

# 27. My hobby

*Hobbies are the most interesting thing in our life, which we live and enjoy in our leisure hours.*
*Hobbies enliven, enhances and instills enthusiasm in us, to work beyond the boundaries, to live a fuller and soothing life in the midst of one's perspective of beauty redefined..*
*In this context, I like to spend my leisure hours in sleeping, as it gives me, peace of mind and rejuvenates my spirit, besides listening to soft 90s music, which are my favourite ones...*
*I listen to best notes whenever I'm low or feel down and sleep engrossed, aftermath in my free time ,*
*which I love to, as while listening to music and trying to get some sleep, with my eyes closed, I feel bliss and ecstatic delight, free from worldly tantrums and hullaballo and I'm in a state of completeness and communication with God.*
*This is the most exotic as well as warming feeling, so I love my hobby and try to be faithful in pursuing it, almost everyday, finding solace and solidarity in sleep.. besides spending hours in household chores and some bit of writing as well..*
*By: Poetry Khakholia Mundra*
*Insta I'd : _befikr_lafz*

# 28. I'm not perfect

*I'm not perfect yet..*
*Yet, I want someone to hold me, love me and*
*live with me with all my*
*flaws and foils...*
*Life would become beautiful and attractive*
*only with your presence, for, your absence kills me.*
*My only abode is your heart, where I dwell*
*every second, cherishing beauty, your charms*
*and you enriching me with all my shortcomings..., for all I know, you are*
*with me, in my worst and*
*whirlpools, never let me drown, but if ever, then shall, drown in your*
*arms loving you forever and ever.*
*For all you are to me*
*my love, I'm not perfect yet I love you more and more, than ever and ever..*
*By: Poetry Khakholia Mundra*
*Insta I'd: _befikr_lafz*

# 29. Priority

*In life, priority is a very significant word, having a pivotal role in our everyday lives...*
*If we work on priority basis, then things , life and people would all run smoothly.. That's why,*
*I always make sure to do my task on a priority basis..*
*Since I have two children so firstly, I leave all work aside, and make food for them so whenever they are hungry they eat and can get back to their works or they get food at proper time, and not eat junk or starve either...*
*Then I finish up with my husband's chores so that he doesn't get annoyed with me ...*
*And then the house and household chores..*
*Last but not the least I prioritise myself atleast for half an hour and do what makes me happy,*
*and eventually if I'm happy, then the whole family will be happy, this what I believe, for that, home is build on the strong pillars of both the housemates.., however, a woman builds castle for her family and children...*
*And very many times, we woman, forget to give any importance to ourselves.. We are not in the list itself, it's we who avoid our own choices and interests, and leave aside our own poor self...*
*Hence everything should be prioritised so that life becomes easier, stronger smoother and smoother and not haphazard, unorganised or indiscriminate, vibes being the gratifying positivity of optimism and occults...*

*By: Poetry Khakholia Mundra*
*Insta I'd: _befikr_lafz*

# 30. My mother my soul

*This is quite complicated question as we are surrounded by so many loved ones and all are pretty well important and necessary, but still if i have to choose that one person, i shall mention, will be none other than my mother..*
*Yes my mother is the most important person in my life, without whom i can't think to live and believe in me also that, writing is all endowed and blessed by her so she's my ideal, idol and inspiration...,and all for what I'm today, without her, my life wouldn't be living for me ...*
*Though, i seldom express this to my mother, that, how much important and indispensable she is to me, shows my wrath and fear, but love her as much as, she does her other children too.*
*But then, i ofter see her eyes melts in tears for my pain, my sufferings however hard, i try or she hides, but down the memory lane, i cherish this beauty of her..,who only wants my happiness, my wellbeing my upliftment in all the regimes of life..*
*And that, what she does, i veil, but my heart knows she loves me more and I love her more everyday, not for what she does always, but for being my mother, the bestest one God gave me, also for being there for me, always and for feeling my pain as hers..., trying all measures to protect and privilege me.*
*I strongly believe that a mother can give everything to her children, still she can't fight with their destiny, with karma and there lies her hidden concern to do and go beyond all deeds and dedication...*
*By: Poetry Khakholia Mundra*

POETRY KHAKHOLIA MUNDRA

*Insta I'd: _befikr_lafz*

Printed by Libri Plureos GmbH in Hamburg,
Germany